This Journal Belongs To

....

Location

Date

Weather conditions

Accompanied by

Birds seen and time spotted

Bird details / behaviour and worth noting

Location

Date

Weather conditions

Accompanied by

Birds seen and time spotted

Bird details / behaviour and worth noting

Location

Date

Weather conditions

Accompanied by

Birds seen and time spotted

Bird details / behaviour and worth noting

Location

Date

Weather conditions

Accompanied by

Birds seen and time spotted

Bird details / behaviour and worth noting

Location

Date

Weather conditions

Accompanied by

Birds seen and time spotted

Bird details / behaviour and worth noting

Location

Date

Weather conditions

Accompanied by

Birds seen and time spotted

Bird details / behaviour and worth noting

Location

Date

Weather conditions

Accompanied by

Birds seen and time spotted

Bird details / behaviour and worth noting

Location

Date

Weather conditions

Accompanied by

Birds seen and time spotted

Bird details / behaviour and worth noting

Location

Date

Weather conditions

Accompanied by

Birds seen and time spotted

Bird details / behaviour and worth noting

Location

Date

Weather conditions

Accompanied by

Birds seen and time spotted

Bird details / behaviour and worth noting

Location

Date

Weather conditions

Accompanied by

Birds seen and time spotted

Bird details / behaviour and worth noting

Location

Date

Weather conditions

Accompanied by

Birds seen and time spotted

Bird details / behaviour and worth noting

Location

Date

Weather conditions

Accompanied by

Birds seen and time spotted

Bird details / behaviour and worth noting

Location

Date

Weather conditions

Accompanied by

Birds seen and time spotted

Bird details / behaviour and worth noting

Location	Date

Weather conditions	Accompanied by

Birds seen and time spotted

Bird details / behaviour and worth noting

Location

Date

Weather conditions

Accompanied by

Birds seen and time spotted

Bird details / behaviour and worth noting

Location

Date

Weather conditions

Accompanied by

Birds seen and time spotted

Bird details / behaviour and worth noting

Location

Date

Weather conditions

Accompanied by

Birds seen and time spotted

Bird details / behaviour and worth noting

Location

Date

Weather conditions

Accompanied by

Birds seen and time spotted

Bird details / behaviour and worth noting

Location

Date

Weather conditions

Accompanied by

Birds seen and time spotted

Bird details / behaviour and worth noting

Location

Date

Weather conditions

Accompanied by

Birds seen and time spotted

Bird details / behaviour and worth noting

Location

Date

Weather conditions

Accompanied by

Birds seen and time spotted

Bird details / behaviour and worth noting

Location

Date

Weather conditions

Accompanied by

Birds seen and time spotted

Bird details / behaviour and worth noting

Location

Date

Weather conditions

Accompanied by

Birds seen and time spotted

Bird details / behaviour and worth noting

Location

Date

Weather conditions

Accompanied by

Birds seen and time spotted

Bird details / behaviour and worth noting

Location

Date

Weather conditions

Accompanied by

Birds seen and time spotted

Bird details / behaviour and worth noting

Location

Date

Weather conditions

Accompanied by

Birds seen and time spotted

Bird details / behaviour and worth noting

Location

Date

Weather conditions

Accompanied by

Birds seen and time spotted

Bird details / behaviour and worth noting

Location

Date

Weather conditions

Accompanied by

Birds seen and time spotted

Bird details / behaviour and worth noting

Location

Date

Weather conditions

Accompanied by

Birds seen and time spotted

Bird details / behaviour and worth noting

Location

Date

Weather conditions

Accompanied by

Birds seen and time spotted

Bird details / behaviour and worth noting

Location

Date

Weather conditions

Accompanied by

Birds seen and time spotted

Bird details / behaviour and worth noting

Location

Date

Weather conditions

Accompanied by

Birds seen and time spotted

Bird details / behaviour and worth noting

Location

Date

Weather conditions

Accompanied by

Birds seen and time spotted

Bird details / behaviour and worth noting

Location

Date

Weather conditions

Accompanied by

Birds seen and time spotted

Bird details / behaviour and worth noting

Location

Date

Weather conditions

Accompanied by

Birds seen and time spotted

Bird details / behaviour and worth noting

Location

Date

Weather conditions

Accompanied by

Birds seen and time spotted

Bird details / behaviour and worth noting

Location

Date

Weather conditions

Accompanied by

Birds seen and time spotted

Bird details / behaviour and worth noting

Location

Date

Weather conditions

Accompanied by

Birds seen and time spotted

Bird details / behaviour and worth noting

Location

Date

Weather conditions

Accompanied by

Birds seen and time spotted

Bird details / behaviour and worth noting

Location

Date

Weather conditions

Accompanied by

Birds seen and time spotted

Bird details / behaviour and worth noting

Location

Date

Weather conditions

Accompanied by

Birds seen and time spotted

Bird details / behaviour and worth noting

Location

Date

Weather conditions

Accompanied by

Birds seen and time spotted

Bird details / behaviour and worth noting

Location

Date

Weather conditions

Accompanied by

Birds seen and time spotted

Bird details / behaviour and worth noting

Location

Date

Weather conditions

Accompanied by

Birds seen and time spotted

Bird details / behaviour and worth noting

Location

Date

Weather conditions

Accompanied by

Birds seen and time spotted

Bird details / behaviour and worth noting

Location

Date

Weather conditions

Accompanied by

Birds seen and time spotted

Bird details / behaviour and worth noting

Location

Date

Weather conditions

Accompanied by

Birds seen and time spotted

Bird details / behaviour and worth noting

Location

Date

Weather conditions

Accompanied by

Birds seen and time spotted

Bird details / behaviour and worth noting

Location

Date

Weather conditions

Accompanied by

Birds seen and time spotted

Bird details / behaviour and worth noting

Location

Date

Weather conditions

Accompanied by

Birds seen and time spotted

Bird details / behaviour and worth noting

Location

Date

Weather conditions

Accompanied by

Birds seen and time spotted

Bird details / behaviour and worth noting

Location

Date

Weather conditions

Accompanied by

Birds seen and time spotted

Bird details / behaviour and worth noting

Location

Date

Weather conditions

Accompanied by

Birds seen and time spotted

Bird details / behaviour and worth noting

Location

Date

Weather conditions

Accompanied by

Birds seen and time spotted

Bird details / behaviour and worth noting

Location

Date

Weather conditions

Accompanied by

Birds seen and time spotted

Bird details / behaviour and worth noting

Location

Date

Weather conditions

Accompanied by

Birds seen and time spotted

Bird details / behaviour and worth noting

Location

Date

Weather conditions

Accompanied by

Birds seen and time spotted

Bird details / behaviour and worth noting

Location

Date

Weather conditions

Accompanied by

Birds seen and time spotted

Bird details / behaviour and worth noting

Location

Date

Weather conditions

Accompanied by

Birds seen and time spotted

Bird details / behaviour and worth noting

Location

Date

Weather conditions

Accompanied by

Birds seen and time spotted

Bird details / behaviour and worth noting

Location

Date

Weather conditions

Accompanied by

Birds seen and time spotted

Bird details / behaviour and worth noting

Location

Date

Weather conditions

Accompanied by

Birds seen and time spotted

Bird details / behaviour and worth noting

Location

Date

Weather conditions

Accompanied by

Birds seen and time spotted

Bird details / behaviour and worth noting

Location

Date

Weather conditions

Accompanied by

Birds seen and time spotted

Bird details / behaviour and worth noting

Location

Date

Weather conditions

Accompanied by

Birds seen and time spotted

Bird details / behaviour and worth noting

Location

Date

Weather conditions

Accompanied by

Birds seen and time spotted

Bird details / behaviour and worth noting

Location

Date

Weather conditions

Accompanied by

Birds seen and time spotted

Bird details / behaviour and worth noting

Location

Date

Weather conditions

Accompanied by

Birds seen and time spotted

Bird details / behaviour and worth noting

Location

Date

Weather conditions

Accompanied by

Birds seen and time spotted

Bird details / behaviour and worth noting

Location

Date

Weather conditions

Accompanied by

Birds seen and time spotted

Bird details / behaviour and worth noting

Location

Date

Weather conditions

Accompanied by

Birds seen and time spotted

Bird details / behaviour and worth noting

Location

Date

Weather conditions

Accompanied by

Birds seen and time spotted

Bird details / behaviour and worth noting

Location

Date

Weather conditions

Accompanied by

Birds seen and time spotted

Bird details / behaviour and worth noting

Location

Date

Weather conditions

Accompanied by

Birds seen and time spotted

Bird details / behaviour and worth noting

Location

Date

Weather conditions

Accompanied by

Birds seen and time spotted

Bird details / behaviour and worth noting

Location

Date

Weather conditions

Accompanied by

Birds seen and time spotted

Bird details / behaviour and worth noting

Location

Date

Weather conditions

Accompanied by

Birds seen and time spotted

Bird details / behaviour and worth noting

Location

Date

Weather conditions

Accompanied by

Birds seen and time spotted

Bird details / behaviour and worth noting

Location

Date

Weather conditions

Accompanied by

Birds seen and time spotted

Bird details / behaviour and worth noting

Location

Date

Weather conditions

Accompanied by

Birds seen and time spotted

Bird details / behaviour and worth noting

Location

Date

Weather conditions

Accompanied by

Birds seen and time spotted

Bird details / behaviour and worth noting

Location

Date

Weather conditions

Accompanied by

Birds seen and time spotted

Bird details / behaviour and worth noting

Location

Date

Weather conditions

Accompanied by

Birds seen and time spotted

Bird details / behaviour and worth noting

Location

Date

Weather conditions

Accompanied by

Birds seen and time spotted

Bird details / behaviour and worth noting

Location

Date

Weather conditions

Accompanied by

Birds seen and time spotted

Bird details / behaviour and worth noting

Location

Date

Weather conditions

Accompanied by

Birds seen and time spotted

Bird details / behaviour and worth noting

Location

Date

Weather conditions

Accompanied by

Birds seen and time spotted

Bird details / behaviour and worth noting

Location

Date

Weather conditions

Accompanied by

Birds seen and time spotted

Bird details / behaviour and worth noting

Location

Date

Weather conditions

Accompanied by

Birds seen and time spotted

Bird details / behaviour and worth noting

Location

Date

Weather conditions

Accompanied by

Birds seen and time spotted

Bird details / behaviour and worth noting

Location

Date

Weather conditions

Accompanied by

Birds seen and time spotted

Bird details / behaviour and worth noting

Location

Date

Weather conditions

Accompanied by

Birds seen and time spotted

Bird details / behaviour and worth noting

Location

Date

Weather conditions

Accompanied by

Birds seen and time spotted

Bird details / behaviour and worth noting

Location

Date

Weather conditions

Accompanied by

Birds seen and time spotted

Bird details / behaviour and worth noting

Location

Date

Weather conditions

Accompanied by

Birds seen and time spotted

Bird details / behaviour and worth noting

Location

Date

Weather conditions

Accompanied by

Birds seen and time spotted

Bird details / behaviour and worth noting

Location

Date

Weather conditions

Accompanied by

Birds seen and time spotted

Bird details / behaviour and worth noting

Location

Date

Weather conditions

Accompanied by

Birds seen and time spotted

Bird details / behaviour and worth noting

Location

Date

Weather conditions

Accompanied by

Birds seen and time spotted

Bird details / behaviour and worth noting

Location

Date

Weather conditions

Accompanied by

Birds seen and time spotted

Bird details / behaviour and worth noting

Location

Date

Weather conditions

Accompanied by

Birds seen and time spotted

Bird details / behaviour and worth noting

Location

Date

Weather conditions

Accompanied by

Birds seen and time spotted

Bird details / behaviour and worth noting

Location

Date

Weather conditions

Accompanied by

Birds seen and time spotted

Bird details / behaviour and worth noting

Location

Date

Weather conditions

Accompanied by

Birds seen and time spotted

Bird details / behaviour and worth noting

Location

Date

Weather conditions

Accompanied by

Birds seen and time spotted

Bird details / behaviour and worth noting

Location

Date

Weather conditions

Accompanied by

Birds seen and time spotted

Bird details / behaviour and worth noting

Location

Date

Weather conditions

Accompanied by

Birds seen and time spotted

Bird details / behaviour and worth noting

Printed in Great Britain
by Amazon

32262914R00066